LAUGH IT UP IN
DEER CAMP

LAUGH IT UP IN DEER CAMP

THE BEST "RIBALD" AMERICAN DEER HUNTING HUMOR

COMPILED BY
BRIAN R. PETERSON

WILLOW CREEK PRESS®

Printed in Canada

To Tom Petrie, fearless humor jockey.

INTRODUCTION

My original deer camp was in northern Minnesota, not far from Nevis, home of the Big Muskie, in the Superior National Forest. The housing for the camp was a large summer-use cabin, poorly insulated for winter occupation and extra income for the lake resort owner. The use of the word "resort" in this context is generous as the amenities in more popular resort destinations were not to be found, just a few Lund aluminum rowboats with Evinrude or Johnson motors at exorbitant hourly rates during the short "high season," and a crude fish cleaning shack.

The best was the Spider Web Resort. It had a decent restaurant, sold 3.2 beer, and provided a few thin towels in the cabins. The sleeping accommodations in the cabins were first come, first serve, and for many years, my long commute from Minneapolis earned the swaybacked couch. On one of my last trips north, handmade cardboard signs (Do Not Disturb, No Vacancy) were placed in strategic spots leading to the cabin and a string of tin cans connected from the inside knob to the refrigerator door.

Pranks were and are a big part of the deer camp experience and descriptions of great pranks share this collection. So are jokes, short anecdotes, tall tales, and several stories that require at least two beers. With few exceptions, they have significant regional variations—Ole in the North becomes Bubba in the South—and all touch on the many aspects of deer camp. The question of why men go to a deer camp is never answered completely. Roger Welsch, in his book *Diggin' in & Piggin' Out* believes men disappear with hunting parties so they won't have to eat with children. Another food reason is only in deer camp can you freely wolf groceries banned from home: Twinkies, SPAM, Wonder Bread, Hostess Cupcakes, Little Debbie Snack Cakes, and other treats from the gas station food mart.

Looking back on the days and nights in that camp and hunting an area that was lean on a stable, sizeable deer population, the memories are broken into small pieces. The common thread was the terrific sense of humor that each member of the hunting party brought to camp. Other than a small measure of protocol given differences in age and experience, there were no subjects off-limits to the ribbing that made you strong.

To have a Minnesota Scandinavian collect deer-hunting humor is risky business. Humor is not to be trusted except in small, highly edited doses in the Sons of Kmute lodge. Louis Anderson identified Kmute (pronounced "mute"), the god of Scandinavian humor in his very funny book, *Scandinavian Humor and Other Myths*, and identified Nordic humor as a "rustic search for new places to put 'Uff Da' buttons, stickers, and plaques and in wearing buttons which demand: Kiss me, I'm 1) Swedish, 2) Norwegian, 3) Danish, 4) Finnish, 5) Icelandic, or 6) Most of the Above." Given this background, I want to give fair warning that I reached out far beyond the lodge parking lot for good material and some of the riskier humor is included only to make the unsuspecting reader blow snot. We apologize for any mess while reading and will clean it up while you are at the office or store. Just leave the key under the mat.

The jokes, anecdotes, and personal experiences of friends and other deer campers are meant to refresh memories of that first weekend in November. Deer hunting humor is largely an oral tradition and many of the longer stories within were told and listened to with tears running down my cheeks. I hope these stories and personal tales from ordinary deer hunters will bring you fine recollections of your camp.

THE DRIVE
AS INTENDED

THE DRIVE
IN REALITY

9

"YONKERS"—THAT'S WHAT ELI SLY CALLS

most hunters who visit his Montana ranch. The term has its origins in two hunters he once guided. They were from Yonkers, New York, and were so green they let deer after deer slip by them. The pair seemed incapable of hitting anything beyond 50 yards.

Last season was a particularly frustrating one for Eli. Big deer were in short supply on his ranch, and a dry, warm fall made even dumb forkhorns unapproachable. By mid-season, although some 20 hunters had passed through his gateposts and covered the pastures that sprawled over two counties, only three tags had been filled.

True, there had been opportunities, but few hunters had connected. Reasons had been cited—spooked deer, running deer, out-of-range deer—but at the root of all the muffs and misses lay the inescapable fact that most of the hunters had been, well… Yonkers.

Then one day at a farm auction Eli's date with destiny was heaved on the block, and he recognized it immediately. It was a mounted mule deer head, obviously some snow-bound rancher's attempt at taxidermy. It was moth-eaten and dusty, and had an ear split that revealed the tin bolster inside, and a nose painted brown instead of black. But it had a giant rack. The tobacco-chewing, clod-kicking ranchers and farmers in attendance had a laugh when Eli's bid of a dollar bought the mount.

"What in blazes are you gonna do with that thing?" one of them asked.

Eli just chuckled.

A hunt with Eli always begins as dawn warms and glows on the horizon. His ranch runs east from the corrals and up a dry coulee; then it forks to the south and north, two miles away. Eli always takes the south fork and drives a route that scribes a huge circle past wheat fields, twisting canyons, sparse stands of juniper and ponderosa pine, sandstone ledges, washouts, and sagebrush.

At selected points along this route canyons are glassed, drives are organized, water holes are watched, and hunters are counseled in the ways of mule deer.

There is a place not 100 yards before you get to the fork where a lone juniper has taken root at the base of a steep cut bank 25 yards from the side of the road. That was the spot Eli chose for the decoy deer.

In his cluttered shop Eli unearthed a five-foot piece of threaded steel pipe. He screwed a T on one end, then extended the T six inches on each side with more pipe. With plumber's tape he affixed the T to the wooden plaque in the back of mounted head, and put the contraption in the bed of his pickup, along with a 30-gallon oil drum and a raw hide. After a short ride and a little rigging, he'd be ready for any and all Yonkers.

He rolled the drum to the base of the cut bank and pushed the pipe supporting the mounted head into the soft earth at one end. Then he draped the hide over the drum. From as close as 25 yards away it looked very much like a breathing animal, and one helluva trophy to boot. Eli chuckled once again.

His object was not so much to play a practical joke as to prove a point. Many times he had whispered, "That's a deer," only to have the hunter at his side say, "Where? I don't see any deer," as the animal loped over the hill and out of sight. With that in mind, Eli coached every hunting party the same way. As he and his hunters neared the last stretched of wheat field a few miles before the fork in the road, Eli would mention that a great, gray ghost of a granddaddy buck had been seen near the ranch the day before. Hunters had caught no more than a glimpse of him, and no one had shot, so he was quite sure the animal was still around. "Keep a sharp eye out, now," Eli would warn. "The hunt's not over yet."

The first place he'd stop would be half a mile from the barrel buck, which was in plain view. He would suggest that somebody glass the coulee bottom below. The second stop was 125 yards away from the deer. The road made a slight curve behind a hill that momentarily obscured the deer, and at that point, the decoy again popped into plain view.

"Man alive! He's big!" he bellowed.

Eli cleared the driver's seat and yelled, "Take a good rest! Take a good rest!"

Jack rolled out one side and Jill tried to exit on the other, but her rifle was wedged across the pickup's door and blocked her way. She kept throwing her weight against the stock, trying to make the rifle bend in the middle.

Meanwhile, Jack had assumed a kneeling position in the dirt. But instead of chambering a shell, he inexplicably hit his clip release, and his clip and shells fell into the grass. He tried to put the clip in backward.

"Man alive, he's big," he said again, his glassed eyes fixed on the animal. The clip slipped from his grasp once more, and this time when he tried to push it back in it finally snapped home. Jack chambered a shell, shouldered the gun, and fired.

BOOM-KERWANG! The almost melodious ring of vibrating metal instantly followed the muzzle blast.

"You missed," Eli yelled. "Shoot him again!"

BOOM-KERWANG! The note jumped an octave higher as the bullet struck a stiffer section of steel.

"I must have him them," Jack said.

"Well, his head is still up… shoot him between the eyes!"

By this time Jill had gathered herself together. She took aim from on offhand position and drilled the mounted head square in the middle of the skull. Sawdust shot out both ears like cartoon smoke from a character who had eaten a too-hot tamale.

There was a puzzled silence for an eternal second. Jack turned, confused, to Eli, whose face was flushed from the strain of suppressed laughter. Tears were streaming down his cheeks. Realization crept across Jack's face.

"Sonofagun," he said. He grinned, looked down, and kicked the dirt.

The statistics Eli amassed during that last half of hunting season were astounding. Out of the 40 hunters he guided, not one saw the deer from half a mile away. At 125 yards, the sun played a major role in the sightings. When the deer was in direct sunlight, nobody missed spotting it. When the weather was cloudy, only about a third of the hunters saw it. And when the low afternoon sun cast a shadow from the lone juniper over the buck, no one saw it, even from 25 yards away!

There were two other memorable incidents. Two hunters pumped 21 rounds into the pinging steel drum before they suspected that something wasn't quite right. Eli's hired man, after having driven past the deer at least seven times, finally saw it at close range. He was on a piece of farm machinery without a gun, so he tried to sneak up on the animal with a tire iron, thinking it was wounded. The deer lost an ear in the ensuing battle. And two persons passed Eli's test with flying colors. One client refused to shoot because the animal had been spotted from a vehicle, and it offended his sense of the chase. A neighbor of Eli's spotted the deer at the 125-yard post, stepped from the truck, shouldered his gun, and after a long pause said, "You ain't gonna sucker me into shooting no stuffed deer."

To a man (and woman), they all took Eli's lesson good-naturedly, and a bit reflective too, for it raised a nagging question: Just how many real deer does one overlook in the course of a season?

One question remains: How did I fare? Well, I never took the test. I happened to arrive at the ranch on a bright, sunny day when Eli wasn't guiding. He had sent some local hunters of his acquaintance into the north wheat field that morning, and they were due back any moment, so he told me about the experiment and we laughed.

Just as we were about to go into the house, the muffled popping of gunfire rolled in from the east. Boom, kerwang, ping, kerpow.

Laugh wrinkles creased Eli's cheeks, and his eyes danced. "Sure got them Yonkers this year," he said, and he chuckled once more.

—*Contributed by Sil Strung*

THREE FRIENDS OF VARIOUS IQS go out deer hunting. The first one goes out and returns two hours later with a deer. The other two ask how he did it, and he said, "I found the tracks. I followed the tracks. I found the deer. I killed the deer."

The second goes out and returns one hour later with a deer. They ask how he did it and he said, "I found the tracks. I followed the tracks. I found the deer. I killed the deer."

The last hunter goes out and returns two hours later, beaten and bruised. The other two asked what happened and he said, "I found the tracks. I followed the tracks. I got hit by a train."

*"Mom never puts Wild Turkey in **her** chocolate cake."*

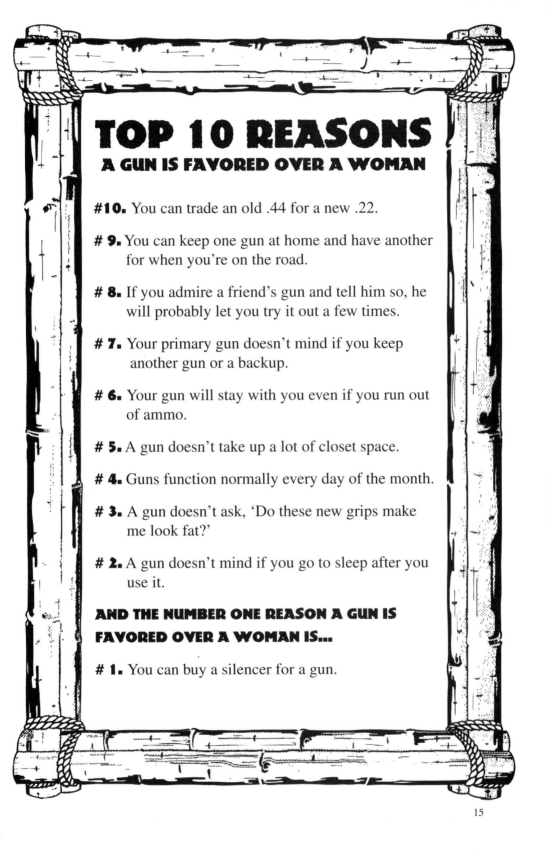

TOP 10 REASONS
A GUN IS FAVORED OVER A WOMAN

#10. You can trade an old .44 for a new .22.

 # 9. You can keep one gun at home and have another for when you're on the road.

 # 8. If you admire a friend's gun and tell him so, he will probably let you try it out a few times.

 # 7. Your primary gun doesn't mind if you keep another gun or a backup.

 # 6. Your gun will stay with you even if you run out of ammo.

 # 5. A gun doesn't take up a lot of closet space.

 # 4. Guns function normally every day of the month.

 # 3. A gun doesn't ask, 'Do these new grips make me look fat?'

 # 2. A gun doesn't mind if you go to sleep after you use it.

AND THE NUMBER ONE REASON A GUN IS FAVORED OVER A WOMAN IS...

 # 1. You can buy a silencer for a gun.

AT O-DARK THIRTY, JENS, the eighty-four-year-old Norwegian patriarch of our deer camp, rousted us from sleep. The night before we had enjoyed a dinner of venison tenderloin, sautéed onions, and baked potatoes washed back with cold beer. Then we moved on to high stakes poker involving nickels, dimes, and quarters. As usual, I squandered a portion of my youngest daughter's college fund. Deer camp at the field mouse Hilton along the banks of the Totagatic River in Northwestern Wisconsin was always an adventure.

From my vantage point entangled in a sleeping bag on the foldout couch, I saw Jens at the stove cooking someting that smelled like bacon. He was a sight in his long johns with a faded and frayed blaze orange stocking cap tilted to one side like some voyageur of old. I hated that hat. He was convinced that dousing it with aged "doe in heat" urine masked the smell of bacon and brought the bucks running. In the 90-degree heat of the cabin, the hat was the only thing any of us could smell. Numerous attempts were made to keep the hat outside, but somehow it always showed up back on his head in the cabin, stink and all.

Jens swore a like a sailor as he cooked, telling us to come eat and get moving before the season was over.

"Dere will be plenty of time for sleeping when you're dead," he barked.

Bodies started moving and hot and black coffee was poured. The radio crackled the weather report. Some pulled on clothes while others pulled off clothes. There was much confusion, noise, and flatulence. It was truly a deer camp morning. It was only the second day of season, so we didn't have the routine down yet. By day three, things would be much worse.

I was called to the truck so we could drive out and drop off hunters at various locations through the woods. Jens had the rocking chair stand. He has hunted out of that stand every morning of deer season for the last ten years. I can only remember him killing one buck from it. But he seemed happy and always saw deer and other critters while sitting in the rocking chair under the great white pine on top of a knoll next to the river. It was a nice place to take a nap as well, as there were usually no deer around to bother him.

We pulled up to where Jens got out and walked to his stand. "Do you want some help?" I asked.

"Hell no! Do ya tink I am too old ta do dis on my own? Well, let me tell you someting, I was shooting deer when you was yust a twinkle in your daddy's eye and I will be shooting deer when you're sitting in a diaper drooling in da old folk's home. Where's my gun?"

I held it in my hand. "Right here. Do you have your flashlight?"

"Damn right I do. It's in my pocket... must be the other pocket. What da hell! Here it is."

"Jens, where are your glasses?"

"Oh, for da holy crap! Dey got all steam up when I came back into da cabin from taking a leak dis morning. De're sitting on da back of da sink. It's okay. I don't need them. Probably won't see a deer anyway. If I shoot, you hear me and come on over den. I may need you to hold my gun while I drag out da big buck," he instructed. "And be quiet going into your stand this morning. Yesterday I tink day heard you all da way down in da cities for da Chrissake!"

Off he went into the darkness. Jens cursed himself for his forgetfulness, flashlight shining all over the place and breaking brush like a bull moose in rut. He was having a grand time.

My day was uneventful. I saw a few does and they say you can't eat antlers, but I would like to hang my tag on some before I die. By sunset I'd had enough and was looking forward to hearing how the others had done. Jens was first.

"You won't never believe what happened to me in da rocking chair. I wouldn't believe it myself if I hadn't been dere in person." Jens always had a way with words.

"I suppose you're going to tell us you got laid by a wood fairy."

"Hell no! If dat were da case, I would still be out dere. Dead, probably."

Jens took a sip from his can of Hamm's. He had a serious look about him. Or was it the glow of the campfire on his face? A hush settled over those of us gathered by the fire. I wondered what could have happened to the old man.

Jens was a keen observer of the natural world and a woodsman of the first order. He had killed more deer, caught more trout, and spent more time in the woods than all of us put together. But he had an air about him now that I had never observed before. He was serious. He wasn't about to tell a joke. Certainly someting big had happened. This is the stuff that deer camp legends are made from. I leaned forward so as to not miss a word.

"Well, I was yust sitting dere and watching for da big buck, ya know. It had been light for about an hour already. I guess about eight thirty or so. You know it vas a real quiet morning," he said before taking another pull.

"Every so often I tought I heard someting movin' behind me. A sneaky buck or someting, I tought. I peek around da tree but didn't see noting, ya know. So I yust sat dere waiting 'cause I know dat big buck is coming by dere one of dese years if I wait.

"Den I heard dat damn noise again, yust a lil' scratching noise. Like a deer pawing da leaves or someting, but now it was really close. I tought I vould be ready for him if he didn't smell me but he wouldn't 'cause I got dat doe pee on my hat, ya know. You guys always laugh, but I tought who will be laughing now when I shoot dis big SOB.

"About dat time I heard scratching again, but dis time it seemed like it might be above me. Yust how tall is dat damn buck, I wondered. I didn't know what to tink, so I yust sat real still and knew dat SOB would be coming into view pretty soon. But I know my hearing ain't dat good, ya know," He paused and took another sip from the can.

"Den someting fell on my head. It looked like a lil' pine cone when it bounced off my hat, but I couldn't see it on da ground. Den I got another one. Plunk! Right on top of my head and den another. I didn't know what da hell was going on or what dat buck might be doing but figured it vas time to look.

"I leaned to my left and looked up into da branches of dat white pine. My hat fell down so I had to raise it up, and yust as I did so, one of dem landed in my eye. Of all da damn tings! I wiped it from my eye and it was warm and kind of dry and sticky, too, for da Chrissake. Witout my glasses I wasn't sure what da hell it was. All I knew was dat I wasn't lettin go of it and I didn't tink it was from a deer.

"Den I looked up and dere in a branch about 15 feet above my head was da biggest damned quill-pig I ever seen." (In these parts, a quill-pig is the name for a porcupine.) "He was crapping right on my head for what da hell!

"Dat goddamn quill-pig had dropped a turd right in my eye for da Chrissake! I tink he had a bombsight on his ass or someting."

Jens reached into a fold of his doe-pee orange stocking cap and pulled out a small object. "Dis one of his turds right here. In case you guys didn't believe me," he said as he held it up between his forefinger and thumb for all to witness. Behold, a porcupine turd.

Beer shot out of my nostrils. Others spilled theirs and were rolling about the fire like some pagan ritual, overcome with laughter. Never in our combined years of deer hunting had anyone ever been soiled by a Boone and Crockett-class porcupine with a bombsight on his ass while sitting in their deer stand.

May Jens, the man, the legend, the human porcupine turd-target, be with us in deer camp for many more years to come.

—*Contributed by Mike Bartz*

TYPES OF ANTLERS

ANTLERS ARE NOT OFTEN USED FOR FIGHTING OTHER MALE DEER OR TO PROD A LAZY DOE FROM HER BED TO POSE FOR A NATURE CONSERVANCY FIELD TRIP. ANTLERS ARE FOR DISPLAY. A BIG RACK REASSURES THE HAREM THAT THEY HAVE CHOSE THE "MAN." POSSESSING A GOOD RACK IS A LOT LIKE OWNING AN IPHONE. A HUGE RACK IS LIKE OWNING AN IPHONE, AN IPOD, AND A CUTE PUPPY.

BUTTON BUCK

SPIKE BUCK

4 POINT BUCK
(2 POINT WEST COUNT)

8 POINT BUCK
(4 POINT WEST COUNT)

THE NEVIS BUCK

Artwork contributed by J. Angus "Sourdough" McLean

A CARLOAD OF HUNTERS went looking for a place to hunt and pulled into a farmer's yard. The driver went up to the farmhouse to ask permission to hunt on his land. The old farmer said, "Sure you can hunt, but would you do me a favor? That old mule over there is 20 years old and sick with cancer, but I don't have the heart to kill her. Would you do it for me?"

The driver said, "Sure," and headed for the car. Walking back, however, he decided to pull a trick on his hunting buddies. He got into the car and when they asked if the farmer said it was okay, he said, "No, we can't hunt here, but I'm going to teach that old cuss a lesson." With that, he rolled down his window, stuck his gun out and blasted the mule. "There, that will teach him!"

A second shot rang out from the passenger side and one of his hunting buddies shouted, "I got the cow!"

ONE NIGHT DURING THE DEER HUNTING season, a police officer was staking out a rowdy country bar for possible DUI violations. At closing time, he saw a hunter tumble out of the bar, trip on the curb, and try his keys in five different cars before he found his. He sat in the front seat fumbling around with his keys for several minutes. All the other deer hunters left the bar and drove off. Finally he started his engine and began to pull away. The police officer was waiting for him. He stopped the driver, read him his rights and administered the Breathalyzer test. The results showed a reading of 0.00. The puzzled officer demanded to know how that could be. The deer hunter replied, "Tonight I'm the designated decoy."

TWO HUNTERS CHARTERED A PILOT to fly them into the far north for deer hunting. They were quite successful in their venture and bagged six big bucks. The pilot came back, as arranged, to pick them up.

They started loading their gear into the plane, including the six deer. The pilot objected and said, "This plane can only take four of your deer. You'll have to leave two behind."

The hunters argued with him. The year before they had shot six and the pilot had allowed them to put all aboard. The plane was the same model and capacity. Reluctantly, the pilot finally permitted them to put all six aboard. When he attempted to take off and leave the valley, the little plane could not make it and they crashed into the wilderness.

Climbing out of the wreckage, one hunter said to the other, "Do you know where we are?"

"I think so," replied the other hunter. "This is about the same place where we crashed last year."

WHEN I WAS A YOUNG MARRIED MAN, I went on a hunting trip without my new wife. My brother, Tim, his wife and I stayed with a farm family in eastern Minnesota and hunted in the hills surrounding their farm. Tim decided to get me in a little bit of trouble. He hid a pair of women's panties scented with perfume in my duffel bag. It was pretty dainty, lacy stuff that my wife would never have worn. When I was home from the trip and unpacked, this pair of women's panties fell out of my bag. My wife wanted to know where they had come from, and right now. I explained and she believed me. For reasons not known to me, the marriage is still going strong.

—*Contributed by Ralph Schultz*

A FATHER AND SON GO OUT HUNTING for the first time. The father says, "Stay here and be very quiet. I'll be across the field." A few minutes later, the father hears a bloodcurdling scream and runs back to his son.

"What's wrong?" the father asked. "I told you to be quiet."

"I was quiet when the snake slithered across my feet," said the son. "I was quiet when the bear breathed down my neck. I didn't move a muscle when the skunk climbed over my shoulder. I closed my eyes and held my breath when the wasp stung me. I didn't cough when I swallowed the gnat. I didn't cuss or scratch when the poison oak started itching. But when the two chipmunks crawled up my pant legs and said, 'Should we eat them here or take them with us?' I just panicked."

DAVE AND FRED WERE OUT DEER HUNTING and, as usual, got lost. Dave told Fred, "Don't panic. I learned what to do in case this happens. You're supposed to shoot up into the air three times and someone will hear you and come with help."

"Okay," says Fred, and he shoots three times into the air. They wait for an hour and no one shows up. So they shoot three times again and still no one shows up. Bewildered they try this again and again for the next couple of hours. Fred starts to look a little worried, then he shouts "It better work this time. We're down to our last three arrows."

"I've always said a boy can learn more on a
trip like this than he could in school any day!"

NOW PLAYING
SECOND WEEK OF DEER CAMP
by Da Yoopers
Copyright ©1987 by Joe Potila and Jim DeCaire
www.dayoopers.com

Hey there goes one (BANG)! Hey you shot my
cow!

It's the second week of deer camp
I got a swollen head
I'm lying with the dustballs
Underneath the bed
An icy breeze is blowing
Into the tongue and groove
My pants are frozen to the floor
And I'm too sick to move
I didn't drink so many
Just thirty cans of beer
It musta been that last shot
That put me under here

REFRAIN
It's the second week of deer camp
And all the guys are here
We drink play cards and shoot the bull
But never shoot no deer
The only time we leave the camp

Is when we go for beer
The second week of deer camp
Is the greatest time of year

I remember playing poker
That weasel musta won
He's wearing my new swampers
And sleeping with my gun
He's snoring like a chainsaw
The camp smells like a dump
Someone's dirty underwear
Is hanging on the pump
Mickey's in the woodbox
Weener's on the stove
His flannel shirt is smoking
I wonder if he knows

REFRAIN

Beadle's crawling through the door
I think he got frostbite
He passed out in the outhouse
And he's been there since last night
Goofus stumbled through the door
He says he got a buck
He was coming from the wayside
And hit it with his truck
Musty cracked a beer and said
Let's celebrate
Goofus caught the first buck
Since 1968

THE MARRIAGE BETWEEN THE ELDERLY
farmer and his young wife was not working out, so the farmer consulted his doctor for advice.

"The next time you're down in the field plowing and feel a yearning for your wife." Said the doctor, "don't wait until lunch time or the end of the day. Quit what you're doing and go to the house."

"I tried that," said the farmer. "By the time I get to the house, I am so tuckered out, it's no use."

The doctor thought for a minute. "Take your rifle with you when you leave the house in the morning and when you feel the urge, shoot the rifle and have her come to you."

A few weeks later the two men met on the street. "How did it work out?" asked the doctor.

"Fine for the first three days," said the farmer. "Then deer hunting season opened and I haven't seen her since."

TWO HUNTERS HAVE GONE DEER HUNTING
every winter for years without success. Finally, they have a fool-proof plan. They got an authentic female deer costume and learned the mating call of a female deer. The plan was to hide in the costume, lure the buck, then come out of the costume shooting. They set themselves up on the edge of a clearing, donned their costume, and began to give the deer love call.

Before long, their call was answered and a huge buck came crashing out of the forest and into the clearing. When the buck was close enough, the hunter in front said, "Okay, let's get out and get him." After a moment that seemed like an eternity, the hunter in the back shouted, "The zipper is stuck! What are we going to do?"

"I'm going to start nibbling grass," said the hunter in front. "But you'd better brace yourself."

SOME BUCKS SEEMED DESTINED TO DIE.

Sam had taken plenty of bucks with a bow, but the one he remembers most vividly he owes to a squirrel. Sam was watching a field from his tree stand along a woods edge one afternoon, when a squirrel began pestering him from a nearby tree. Sam put up with the nuisance for a while and then took a shot at the squirrel to shut it up. The arrow missed and sailed out of sight through the woods. Some time later, Sam spied a nice eight-pointer in the woods, coming along a trail that would take it into the field, too far away for a shot. Suddenly the buck stopped, sniffed at something, then spooked and ran right toward Sam's tree. It slowed to a walk as it approached, giving Sam an easy 20-yard shot.

After he recovered the buck, Sam backtracked it to see what had spooked it. He found the arrow he had shot at the squirrel stuck right in the middle of the trail.

—Contributed by Dan Small @ www.dansmalloutdoors.com

A MAN TAKES HIS WIFE to the Big Horn show. As they strolled through the show enjoying the sights, they noticed a seminar on the life cycle of the deer. This sounded interesting so they went in and joined the seminar already in progress.

About that time, the speaker stated, "A dominant buck may mate 100 or more times in a single season."

The wife's mouth drops open. "Wow, that's more than once a day! You could really learn from these deer."

The man turns to her and says, "Raise your hand and ask him if it was with the same doe."

"I don't even care if I shoot a deer. I'm just going for the solitude."

A FIRST TIME DEER HUNTER BOOKED a hunt with an experienced outfitter. He would be hunting a productive area, but it was filled with grizzly bears. When he got to camp, he insisted that his guide be 60 years old or older. The outfitter thought this was very odd, seeing that the hunter was in his early thirties.

The novice hunter downed a nice buck, but skinning and butchering the deer attracted a big grizzly. The hunter returned to base camp with his clothes shredded, telling the story of being attacked by a bear.

The outfitter wanted to know where his guide was. The hunter said he was still lying in the woods. The outfitter asked him how his clothes got torn, and the hunter said that while they were working on the deer carcass, a grizzly bear had ambushed them.

"I hit the bear with my gun and took off running. As I was running away the guide yelled at me to play dead, that I couldn't outrun a bear. I yelled back that I didn't have to outrun the bear, I just had to outrun him."

A COUPLE OF HUNTERS ARE OUT in the woods when one of them suddenly grabs his chest and falls to the ground. He stops breathing and his eyes roll back in his head. The other hunter whips out his cell phone and calls 911. He gasps to the operator, "I think Frank is dead! What should I do?" The operator, in a calm soothing voice says, "Just take it easy and follow my instructions. First, let's make sure he's dead." There is silence, and then a shot is heard. The man comes back on the line. "Okay, now what?"

AN OLD DEER HUNTER GOES TO HIS DOCTOR
for his yearly physical with his wife along.

When the doctor enters the exam room, he tells the old hunter, "I need a urine sample and a stool sample."

The old duffer, hard of hearing, looks at his wife and yells, "Whats he want?'

His wife yells back, "He wants your underwear."

A WOMAN GOES INTO a sporting goods store to buy a deer rifle. "It's for my husband," she tells the clerk.

"Did he tell what caliber to get?" asked the clerk.

"Are you nuts?" she says. "He doesn't even know I'm gonna shoot him".

A WOMAN IS IN BED WITH HER LOVER who happens to be her husbands best friend. They engage in wild, passionate love for hours and in the quiet afterglow, the phone rings. The wife tells her lover to be very quiet and picks up the phone.

"Hello! Oh hi, honey! I'm really glad you called. Really? I'm so proud of you. Terrific! Thanks for calling, darling. OK. Bye bye."

She hangs up the phone and her lover asks, "Who was that?"

"Oh", she replied. "That was my husband telling me about the great time he's having hunting deer with you."

"I'll bet there's quite a story behind that."

DAVE AND BOB WERE PLAYING CRIBBAGE in Bob's camp trailer the night before the deer opener. A last minute guest joined us, and he arrived with his cowboy hat on.

They had several drinks that night, and Cowboy Bill managed to get himself hopelessly drunk. Bill had a habit that Dave and Harry knew about. He always had to poop first thing in the morning.

As Bill got into bed, Dave and Harry took his hat and put it into the toilet, upside-down. Sure enough, when the alarm went off, Bill darted for the bathroom and pulled the door shut.

He came out and asked "Anyone seen my hat?"

"No," said Dave. "You were wearing it last night. What did you do?"

"I don't know. You guys got me drunk."

"Well," Harry said, "you were wearing it when you went to the john before going to bed."

He went to the bathroom, looked in the toilet, and found his hat along with his morning contribution.

—*Contributed by Dave Richey*

FOUR FRIENDS WENT DEER HUNTING and paired off for the day. That night, one of the hunters returned alone, staggering under the weight of a ten-point buck.

"Where's Harry?"

"He had a stroke of some kind. He's a couple of miles back up the trail."

"You left Harry laying out there and carried the deer back?"

"A tough call," nodded the hunter. "But I figured no one in their right mind is going to steal Harry."

A DEER-HUNTING GUIDE LEADS HIS PARTY

in circles in the mountains and they blame him for getting lost. "You told us you were the best guide in Colorado," they complain. "I am," he said. "But I think we're in Wyoming."

DEER HUNTER 1:

Why do you go hunting without bullets?

DEER HUNTER 2:

Because it's cheaper and the results are the same.

"Now I remember what we forgot!"

SEVERAL YEARS AGO WHEN I GOT MARRIED

to my wife Molly, my uncle Bert flew us down to Texas. I told him that I always wanted to hunt whitetail there so he made it happen. Bert picked us up at the airport and told me war stories about spiders and scorpions. Years before I had a friend who was hunting there and had a mouse come in the blind and run across his foot, followed by a hungry rattlesnake. I imagine my friend left pretty quick.

Having bugs in the blind concerned me and I found a bug bomb. When Bert took me out to the blind, I wanted to pay attention to the hunting rather than to the spiders and scorpions. I opened the door to the blind and set off the bomb, and gave it some time to air out. I climbed in and started my hunt. A little while later I heard what I thought was a bird on the roof, and then another. I didn't know if this was a good or a bad thing. One tried to crawl in the door. They were scorpions. I had disturbed a big nest in the ceiling of the blind. They were crawling outside and falling off. Since there is no field dressing in Texas, I didn't have a knife to stick these scorpions for a later meal or just to save myself.

I propped the door open, took a quick scan, and jumped out of there and squealed like a schoolgirl. I hunted the rest of the day from a tree. When Bert came and picked me up, he asked why I was standing outside the blind, and I told him. The next day, Bert dropped me off at a tree blind on stilts. I climbed the stairs and was ready to shoot off my bug bomb. When I opened to the door, I was staring face to face with a huge barn owl that had several eggs lying in the bottom of the blind, and many regurgitated rodents. I shut the door and got down the stairs as fast as possible to get away from the owl. I found another tree to huddle next to until Bert came back. Texas, especially hunting in Texas, is definitely only for Texans.

—*Contributed by Kent Klineberger*

I WAS ON THE TETON RIVER, where I trapped beaver and mink. It was five or ten below zero, and slush ice ran in the river with shelf ice coming out from the bank about five feet. The river was shallow enough that the water was four inches from the top of my hip boots. One morning I saw a deer across the river. I had a tag so I shot him. He went down and lay there, and I left my gun on one side of the river and waded across. Rather than gutting the deer, I got him on my shoulders and walked him across. There was no sign of life when I picked him up. I was halfway when the hind legs started to jerk. I didn't think much of it for another couple of steps until he jerked his leg out from my grip and got his leg behind my head and started beating on me.

The deer blacked one of my eyes and beat up the back of my head but I couldn't drop him. I walked on across and threw him out on the shelf ice until I managed to cut his throat. He tasted good.

—*Contributed by Rhett Bradford*

BUBBA AND JUNIOR WERE ROAD HUNTING for deer, drinking a couple beers when Bubba said, "Look up thar, Junior, it's a warden roadblock! We're gonna get busted for drinking and hunting!" "Don't worry, Bubba." Junior said, "We'll just pull over, down these beers, peel off the labels and stick 'em on our forehead and stash the bottles under the seat." "Why do that?" said Bubba. Junior answers, "Just let me do the talking." They finished their beers, hid the bottles and labeled their foreheads and when they reached the roadblock, the warden said "You boys been drinking?" "No, sir," said Junior pointing at the labels on their forehead. "We're on the patch."

HOW BUCKS GROW ANTLERS

ANTLERS ARE BONE DISPLAYS ON THE TOP OF MOST ADULT MALE DEER AND, UNLIKE THE HORN OF THE COW, ARE SHED EACH YEAR. THIS DOESN'T MEAN YOU CAN'T SHOOT A COW IF THEY ARE IN SEASON. THE BONE DISPLAYS UNDER BUCKS THAT CLEAR THE BARBED WIRE FENCES ARE AN OBJECT OF PRIDE IN THE ANIMAL KINGDOM. ANTLERS START GROWING EARLY SPRING, FUELED BY TESTOSTERONE, THE MALE HORMONE. IF A WISCONSIN TROPHY HUNTER DOESN'T BLOW OFF THE ANTLERS, THEY WILL NATURALLY BE SHED IN THE WINTER, CAUSING AN UNUSUAL AND OFTEN UNBEARABLE LIGHTNESS OF BEING.

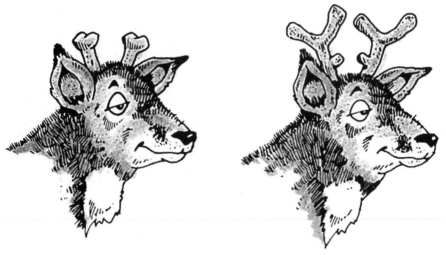

LATE SPRING   SUMMER

40

EARLY FALL

LATE FALL/WINTER

LATE WINTER /EARLY SPRING

Artwork contributed by J. Angus "Sourdough" McLean

IT WAS A CRISP OCTOBER MORNING in Wyoming, the type every mule deer hunter and guide dreamed of. As I panned with my spotting scope, I noticed the distinct antlers of a true prairie giant. This was one of the largest bucks I'd seen in my guiding career, and he had no idea we were there. I pointed him out to Charles, my first client of the season.

We began our stalk, playing the wind and closing the 1500-yard gap between the trophy of a lifetime and us. As we approached from behind the bedded buck, it became clear the shot would be close. The rolling terrain would not allow us to see farther than 40 yards, and the buck was bedded over the next hill.

"You've got the bolt closed and the safety on, right Charles?"

"Yes."

"Is the scope set to low magnification?"

"Yes."

The shot was 25 yards or less, and we definitely had the drop on the buck. His enormous, box-shaped antlers were the first thing visible. The plan was for me to blow on my predator call to get him to stand up and turn broadside. Charles was set for a short kneeling shot and we would celebrate our great fortune in no time.

I blew the predator call and the buck stood up as planned. Then I heard the click of a firing pin finding an empty chamber. "You don't have a shell in the chamber?" I whispered. Charles slowly ran the bolt until it closed on another empty chamber. "You still don't have a shell in the chamber." Click. "You short-stroked the bolt. Take your time. He still hasn't figured out what we are."

Charles frantically ran the bolt again and it was obvious that the rifle was not feeding ammunition into the chamber. The deer vanished as quickly as he had appeared in my spotting scope. I should have asked if he remembered to bring the detachable magazine.

I returned to the truck for the magazine and everything looked to be in working order. However, I noticed a mix of .30-06 cartridges: round-nose, plastic-tipped, and partitioned bullets, each of a different weight. How could I have missed this during sight-in?

Did Charles have a Lazy Susan of ammunition to pick from? It turns out that he'd brought only three rounds of similar ammunition, which had been used during sight-in.

Charles insisted that they all had the same point of impact and that we could continue hunting. As luck would have it, we managed to spot the same buck working up a draw with two smaller bucks. We made our way to the head of the draw and got in position. The first smaller buck emerged with the second smaller buck 10 yards behind him.

"Your buck should be next," I said. "Take your time and hold on the point of his shoulder." The big buck stepped out. "There he is, on the right. Are you on the right one?"

He said he was and took his shot.

The bullet hit 25 yards to the left of the intended buck, almost knocking the first buck in the flank. I'm pretty sure that buck is still running to this day.

Though other opportunities at great deer were unrewarded, Charles' spirits remained high. Most hunters would be discouraged, but not him. Charles was the type of client that has become a rarity. He was on the hunt for the companionship and fun; tagging a good deer would only be a bonus. We traded stories after each unsuccessful stalk and agreed that we needed to be 50 yards or closer before attempting another shot. Charles opted to use his rifle rather than borrow mine. He had used that rifle for years and it had sentimental value.

The sun was getting high on the last morning of the hunt and the deer had been bedded for hours. We decided to head to camp for lunch, but not before we check one last draw on the way back.

"Charles, take a look at the head of that draw. This could be perfect."

Charles decided that was the deer he wanted. He was not the biggest buck we had seen, but more than respectable and the setup seemed ideal. We eased out of sight and began planning yet another stalk.

"Is the magazine in the rifle?"

"Yes."

"Are there shells in the magazine?"

"Yes."

"Do you have all of your ammunition with you?"

"Yes."

I directed Charles to place his crosshairs on a reddish rock on the hill above the deer. When I blew on the predator call, the buck would stand with his shoulder in line with the rock.

"Charles, it's 18 yards to the deer's antlers. You ready?"

"Yes."

"Is the safety off?"

"Yes."

I made one soft blow on the call and the buck stood up. BOOM!

"You shot high, Charles. Shoot again. Hold right on his shoulder."

BOOM!

"Right through his hams, Charles. Hit him again before he can…" And the buck vanished into the next draw. We quickly made our way to a high point just in time to see him run into a dry creek bed and never come out.

"It's okay, Charles. We know where he is. He'll probably lay down right there. Do you have more ammunition?"

"Yes."

Thirty minutes later we located the buck, below us in the dry creek bottom. He was at 22 yards and had no idea we were there. Yes, we had actually managed to get that close again. Charles took careful aim and placed one round between the tops of his antlers, completely missing the body. As the buck tried to stand, I heard Charles say, "That was my last shell."

The deer gained his feet and tried to run for no man's land. My rifle was too far away. "Use your pistol!" Charles yelled.

When something starts running away, you have the uncontrollable urge to chase it. As I closed the gap, the deer picked up speed.

I learned two things that day:

1. A ham-shot mule deer and a Wyoming guide can run at exactly the same speed.

2. A thumb-break holster may as well be Fort Knox if you are sprinting.

There I was, running across the prairie at arms-length from a wild-eyed, wounded deer, and trying to make my holster cough up my revolver. The holster finally conceded and I shoved the pistol against the buck's shoulder and pulled the double-action trigger. The deer dropped and I tripped over his antlers. This launched me across the creek bottom and I slammed into the far bank. Somewhere along the line, my revolver flew out of my hand and nearly obtained geosynchronous orbit. Gravity prevailed and my Smith & Wesson came to rest squarely between my shoulder blades.

I dusted myself off as Charles kept saying how this was the best hunt he'd ever been on. If this was the best, I can't even imagine what the others were like. I took a few pictures and we field dressed our kill. The man who entered my camp known as Charles was leaving as "Cluster Chuck."

Charles hunted with another friend the following year. They saw a small buck go into a pocket of brush and knew it was about to come out the other side. The outfitter instructed him to get ready. When the deer emerged, the outfitter told him to shoot. As the deer ran away, the outfitter's heart sank.

But Cluster Chuck insisted the deer had gone down. The outfitter noticed his rifle was pointed in a completely different direction. Charles had been watching the wrong side of the brush. When a deer came out, he shot it. That buck scored in the mid 190s and was the largest deer that outfitter had ever taken, and from nearly 500 yards away. Chuck had aimed for a 175-yard shot, but killed a Boone & Crockett buck at 500 yards.

HUNTING CAMP
RULES!

#1. Any hunter who gets lost must return to camp at once.

#2. No eating yellow snow.

#3. The "I'm Lost" signal is three shots, 30 seconds apart. Three shots, 10 seconds apart will require your presence at the range.

#4. Obnoxious odors shall be kept in your boots or pants.

#5. All hunting stories must be substantiated by at least two others.

#6. All arguments will be settled by the cook. The cook's word is final and that is that. Signed: the Cook.

#7. No explanations needed when you return to camp without a sock or glove.

#8. Any lighting of farts must be done outdoors.

#9. First timers are not allowed to pee off the front porch.

#10. What happens in deer camp, stays in deer camp. Unless large money is involved.

IN DISPLACED NORWEGIAN ENCLAVES through-
out the Midwest, lutefisk dinners are held during deer season. These
events are usually held in a church basement and are significant
fundraising activities for the congregation. Much has been written
of the taste and traditions of lutefisk, little pro and much con, and
the best description may be contained in a story about two Norwe-
gians talking on Main Street, one pointing to the other's dog and
saying, "Your dog must have worms the way he's licking his butt."

"No," the other replied. "He's been eating lutefisk and trying to
get the taste out of his mouth."

*"That's either one hell of a rub, or
Uncle Charlie hit this tree with his jeep."*

MY HUNTING BUDDIES ARE NOT the greatest hunters in the world. Their ancestors were more likely gatherers instead of hunters, or to be honest, most probably scavengers. Not only do my hunting buddies never kill anything, but they are also adept at raiding whatever you happen to possess in the way of food and gear.

Steve, the bloody limey from London, is the most notorious scavenger of all. He boasts about his ability to travel light, which means getting by on whatever I bring.

Once when we were planning a backpacking trip into Oregon's High Cascade for a buck hunt, Steve announced that he wasn't "going to sleep in any wimpy tent."

"Do tell," I said. "And just what do you intend to employ for accommodations?"

"I'll sleep outside in my jumper (pronounced 'jump-ah')."

I laughed smugly. "That alone will be worth the hike!"

When we finally arrived at our camp beside a quiet lake, Steve had more spring in his step than I did, owing to the fact that he had only packed in his gun, some tea, and the clothes on his back, while I had lugged all of the camp gear I considered necessary.

After I pitched the dome tent and blew up my air mattress, we decided to have dinner and then turn in. I dug out the propane cylinder and the one-burner stove I had packed, and Steve asked if I had a pan he could use to make tea. I grumbled that I needed it for cooking my pork and beans, but gave in and gave him the pan. As I tried to stir the pork and beans that I now had to cook in its can perched atop the three prongs of the one-burner stove, he asked if I was going to eat "all those beans."

I grumbled about English oppression of the Irish, and scooped out the top portion of the beans to him on a plate that I had to provide for him. Logician that he is, he reasoned that I could eat the remaining portion straight from the can. I reached for the can, burned my fingers, and promptly knocked the can into the dirt.

Steve doubled over in laughter, spitting a mouthful of beans on me and spilling a few more off his plate, which he nearly dropped as he grabbed his side.

I went for the can again and burned my fingers for the second time in a span of five seconds. Each time my reflex was to cram my singed fingers into my mouth. After my second attempt at retrieving the can, I stuck dirty fingers in my mouth, causing me to spit with disgust.

By this time, Steve was on the ground in the grips of hysterical laughter, tears streaming from under eyelids that were scrunched shut, perhaps an involuntary reaction to the convulsions he was in, but probably just because he couldn't stand to see any more.

When the can's temperature and my temper had cooled down enough for me to right the can, I was at least consoled that a portion of the beans had not spilled from the can. This, of course, was the portion that had burned black in the bottom of the can. Ah, yes, this was the contentment in the great outdoors for which I had lugged all this weight nearly three miles.

As darkness descended, the mountain air turned cold and mosquitoes starting flying sorties through our camp. About that time, Steve asked, "How much room 'ave you got in that tent?"

Once inside, he complained that the tent was so small he had to "lay with me legs bent up me bum." And the ground was too hard for him to sleep comfortably in his jumper. "Bloody, hell," he moaned. "I think you pitched the tent on a ruddy rock. How about lending me your air mattress since you got a sleeping bag as well?"

The man had endless nerve and he was getting on mine. I gave him the air mattress just to shut him up. Then he complained that it wasn't properly inflated. I told him he was properly inflated, and he soon began to release gas undoubtedly generated by the beans he stole from me. I couldn't help thinking the man ought to work for the government.

The next day I killed a big-bodied four-point buck. Adding injury to insult, because his pack had nothing in it, he got the packing duties.

"I'm sure glad you travel light, Steve," I said as I skipped down the wilderness trail with a mere 30 pounds of gear on my back. "I don't know what I'd do if I had to pack all this gear and a big buck!"

He cursed as he staggered along behind me. All I could make out was something to the effect of "bloody Irish," "ruddy Yanks," and "independence, my bum."

—Contributed by Dewey Delaney

A FELLOW FROM OKLAHOMA went hunting in neighboring Colorado. Late in the afternoon on opening day, the game warden came into his camp and saw a deer he had shot right between the eyes. The warden said, "You sure are a good shot."

"Yeah," replied the non-resident hunter. "We Oklahomans really know how to shoot."

The next day, the game warden returned to the same camp and found a big elk hanging from the rack and that was also shot between the eyes. The warden said, "You boys sure do know how to hunt and shoot."

The man from Oklahoma replied, "I told you we Oklahomans know how to hunt. I'm planning to fill my bear tag tomorrow, too."

The warden wished him well and told him he'd return to see how he did.

The next day the game warden came to the camp where he saw a big bear shot through both front paws and between the eyes. The game warden asked the Oklahoman how he happened to shoot the bear in the hands and he replied, "When that bright light hit his eyes, he covered his face with both hands."

A CITY HUNTER BAGGED A BIG BUCK in the backcountry and just about the time he reached the deer and realized how long a shot he made, the game warden arrived.

"You got a hunting license?"

"No sir. I guess you've caught me."

"Confession is good for the soul, boy. Now I'm going to have to take you into town and file charges. We'll need that deer for evidence."

The game warden and the hunter dragged the 300-pound deer down off the mountain and out to the road where his truck was parked. The hunter thanked the warden for his help and said, "I just remembered. My license is in my back pocket."

"What do you figure this buck weighs...
fifteen hundred, maybe two thousand pounds?"

THE GREATEST THREAT TO OUR HUNTING

heritage may not be habitat destruction, anti-hunters, wolves, or even poison oak. The real threat is hunting video games, because they offer a far better experience than the real thing.

Our family never owned a video game player because my wife Dorey believed the boys would waste too much time playing silly games instead of doing their homework and chores. Finally Dorey got tired of all the whining and begging and gave in. The kids were a little embarrassed that I had whined and begged so much, but they had to admit they learned a valuable lesson—persistence pays off and groveling works wonders. That's knowledge every growing boy should take with him, and never forget once he's married.

Derwood and Darwin bought the predictable football and basketball games, and I grabbed the latest and greatest deer hunting game. The boys would hog the game 24/7 were it not for my creative ways of diverting their attention to their homework and chores, and important jobs like changing the air in my tires.

Once I removed the competition, I was ready to plug in the game. Hunting video games have become more life-like and sophisticated in recent years, but the experience is really nothing like hunting. On the contrary, the video version of hunting is actually enjoyable.

For starters, the video games are way less expensive. A game player is less than half the cost of a deer rifle, and you can get a game cartridge for the price of one box of premium magnum cartridges. And you can use it over and over again without ever getting near a reloading bench. What I wasted on licenses and tags last year would have paid for the game player and a maid to dust it for me.

With video games, there's no closed season or after hours. You can hunt 24-7-365. That means no rolling out of bed at 4 AM and getting soaked to the skin before sunup. You can bag a nice buck without even getting out of bed, and you don't even have to gut it, pack it and skin it.

No matter the season or time of day, you can enjoy the action in a climate-controlled setting. You may have great tracking snow on the screen, but your living room remains toasty. It's rare to get sunburn or a case of frostbite in your family room, and cases of virtual poison oak are almost unheard of. Likewise, few people ever get lost or contract Lyme disease in their living room.

I managed to do some silly things in the video game, like roll my ATV, fall off a cliff, and even shoot my decoy. But they only cost me a few points and nowhere near as goofy as some of the stunts I've pulled in real life, such as slamming my thumb in the pickup door, pitching a tent on an anthill, or realizing a mile down the road that I had left my rifle leaning against my back bumper. Every hunting rig should come with a reset button.

Video games are better than real hunting because you can set the game on "easy" level. Don't like your vehicle? Just go back to the menu, and get yourself a new Powerstroke with a simple pinky stroke. You don't even have to haggle. The video outfitters have much better gear to choose from than the selection in my garage, and it ain't been chewed by rats or my lazy Labradors.

Shopping for your trip? Get real. If you get hungry playing virtual hunting, just waddle over to the fridge or order a pizza. You can even drink beer while you're playing, and you can pause the hunting game and check in on the football game. And when the pizza and beer takes its toll, you can enjoy the comforts of a modern bathroom instead of hunkering in knee-deep snow.

I'm truly convinced that hunting video games are far superior to actual hunting. At least until Dorey asks me to turn the game off, put down my beer, and take out the garbage. The "mute" button won't work on that woman, so I guess I'll see you in hunting camp.

—*Contributed by Dewey Delaney*

What Do Deer Do All Year LONG

SPRING:

JUST LIKE IN THE DISNEY MOVIES, BAMBI IS BORN IN THE SPRING AND THE FURRY DARLING ON WOBBLY LEGS FROLICS IN FIELDS OF FLOWERS WITHOUT A CARE IN THE WORLD OTHER THAN THE THOUGHT OF LOSING THEIR SPOTS. IN THE LATE SPRING, ELDERS TEACH THEM REPUBLICAN FAMILY VALUES. THE YOUNG REBELS WHO ARE UNABLE TO ABSORB THE LESSONS MOVE ON TO A MORE LIBERAL, URBAN ENVIRONMENT.

SUMMER

SUMMER: DEER *GOOF* ALL SUMMER AND CAN BE FOUND (NOT SHOT, EXCEPT IN THE WARDEN'S BACKYARD) SUNNING ON OPEN EXPOSURES. URBAN DEER EAT THE ROSEBUSHES AND GARDENS OF WELL-MEANING ENVIRONMENTALISTS, AND WILD DEER STOCK UP ON MORE ORGANIC GROCERIES. DEER LIVING IN NATIONAL PARKS ARE REQUIRED TO POSE FOR GOLDEN PASSPORT HOLD-ERS ON A SET SCHEDULE OR RISK LOSING THEIR GARBAGE DUMP PASSES.

FALL:

AFTER THE FIRST HARD FROST, DEER PREPARE FOR THE LONG WINTER
AHEAD. NATIONAL PARK DEER ARE REQUIRED TO TIDY UP THE PUBLIC
AREAS AND THEIR LEAF PILES ARE TORCHED UNDER SPECIAL NATIONAL
PARK SERVICE ORIGINAL OCCUPANTS BURN PERMITS. ONCE THE CLEANUP
IS COMPLETE, DEER THOUGHTS, HOWEVER SIMPLE, TURN TOWARD LOVE,
UNGULATE STYLE, BEHIND THE RANGER STATION.

WINTER:

THE DEER THAT MADE IT THROUGH
THE HUNTING SEASON WITH LIMBS
STILL ATTACHED CELEBRATE THE
HOLIDAYS, ALONG WITH THE YOUNG-
STERS RETURNING HOME FROM
PETA ROADSIDE PETTING PARKS. ALL
SHARE THE TRADITIONAL HOLIDAY
FOODS SUCH AS ROASTED ACORNS,
AND THE NEW YEAR IS RUNG IN WITH
MIND-ALTERING MUSHROOMS AND
RESOLUTIONS TO BE MORE CAREFUL
WHEN CROSSING THE HIGHWAY.

Artwork contributed by J. Angus "Sourdough" McLean

TWO BOWHUNTERS WERE OUT ENJOYING
deer season in rural Alabama near a blacktop highway. A huge
buck walked by and one hunter drew his bow and took careful aim.

Before he could release his arrow, his friend pointed at a
funeral procession passing on the road below their stand. The
hunter slowly let off the pressure on his bow, took off his hat,
bowed his head, and closed his eyes in prayer.

His friend was amazed. "Wow, that is the most thoughtful and
touching thing I have ever seen. You are the kindest man I've ever
known."

The hunter shrugged. "Yeah, well, we were married for 35
years."

TWO HUNTERS FROM KENTUCKY were dragging
their dead deer back to their car. A hunter from Tennessee met
them, who also pulled along his deer.

"Hey, I don't want to tell you how to do something but it's
much easier if you drag the deer in the other direction. Then the
antlers won't dig into the ground."

After the Tennessee hunter left, the two from Kentucky decided
to give his advice a try. A little while later one hunter said, "You
know, that guy was right. This is a lot easier!"

"Yeah, but we're getting farther from the truck," said the other.

IF A DEER HUNTER SAYS SOMETHING IN
the woods and his wife is not around, is he still wrong?

A GROUP OF DEER HUNTERS WERE IN CAMP

when they realized they were running low on supplies and appointed Jake to go to town for provisions. Jake went into the general store and bought a case of whiskey, a keg of beer, and two loaves of bread. When he returned to the deer shack, the group looked in his truck and asked, "Damn, Jake what are we going to do with all that bread?"

"Nobody shot him. He got into some of our coffee and just keeled over."

MY GRANDMOTHER ALWAYS USED TO LOOK

out for me when I played games like Cowboys and Indians with my uncles, who were proficient hunters and had a knack for waiting in ambush. Whenever I got into a perilous predicament in close proximity to Chief Wannaswatu, Grandma would bark the warning: "Chiggers, Dewey!"

I figured that chiggers were an unseen danger and not for real, like the goblins in Grandma's favorite poetry book that would get you if you don't watch out. As I got older, I put chiggers in the category with the snipe I was invited to hunt that never materialized. In my adult life, I added elk to this category of mythical creatures that tormented me.

The local guys at the Oregon Department of Fish and Wildlife told me that snipe and elk really do exist and that hunters actually bag some. I have never believed them, so when my son Darwin drew a tag for a youth deer hunt in Douglas County and ODFW sent a letter that included a warning about chiggers in the hunt area, I didn't believe that, either.

The beastly bugs came to Oregon when turkeys were imported from the south. As if I needed another motive to shoot turkeys.

After our first hunt there, we came home looking like we had a case of the measles from the armpits down. These hateful creatures hopped on our hunting boots and then migrated north, looking for warmer climates. The mites have brains smaller than a drop of beer and easily get confused. When they reach a part of the body where limbs diverge, they run back and forth between the limbs, biting in frustration.

Eventually they ran out of real estate when they reached the barrier known as the Fruit of the Loom waistband. They circumnavigated our torsos, sampling the fare and left us with a ring of red, itching, burning bumps I called the ring of fire.

When we returned to the area for our next hunt, Darwin and I were determined to protect ourselves from these blood-sucking bugs. After the compulsory stop at a drive-through for breakfast burritos, we arrived at the hunt area and wrapped our clothing cuffs in camo duct tape. We hoped that the duct tape would provide a barrier from the bugs, and if they tried to cross it, they might get stuck on it like fly paper. I added a few extra wraps for good measure, and soon we looked like camouflaged mummies.

Unfortunately, all the tape did was make it more difficult for the chiggers that found their way in to find their way out. Much like a roach motel, chiggers checked in, but they didn't check out. We had effectively made ourselves human chigger hotels. So when we got back in our rig and headed for home, we became little more than meals on wheels.

It could have been a nightmare if we had brought the pests home, but it would have been gratifying to get even with my Labradors, Love and Money, for their long history of bringing biting bugs into my bungalow. Thankfully, it didn't come to that. The breakfast burritos kicked in, and noxious gases fumigated the chiggers trapped inside our trousers.

—Contributed by Dewey Delaney

A TROPHY BUCK HUNTER TOOK HIS WIFE
and mother-in-law on his annual deer hunt. Late on the first day, the hunter's wife noticed that her mother was missing and both set out to find her. In an open field not too far from the camp, they came upon a frightful sight. His mother-in-law was standing against a large tree and a trophy buck in full rut stood facing her.

The wife cried, "What can we do to help my mother?"

"Not a thing," her husband said. "That trophy buck got himself into this mess, let him get himself out of it."

OBLIGATORY BUMPER STICKERS:

WHAT HAPPENS IN DEER CAMP STAYS IN DEER CAMP

BOWHUNTERS HAVE LONGER SHAFTS

I LiKE **BIG** RacKS

I'm in a Rut!

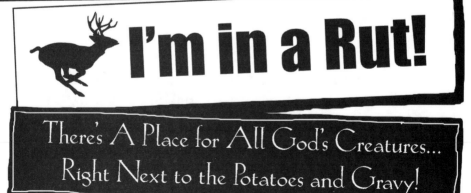

There's A Place for All God's Creatures... Right Next to the Potatoes and Gravy!

61

MY SCHEME WAS SIMPLE ENOUGH:

Set up base camp for Oregon's High Cascade buck season on the edge of the Rogue-Umpqua Divide Wilderness, hunt the wilderness on opening weekend, and if unsuccessful, leave the tent trailer set up there until the following weekend, at which time we would repeat the same exercise.

The plan was working perfectly. My son Darwin and I didn't see a darned deer the whole darned weekend. We distracted ourselves playing Survivor Man, building a lean-to shelter using only our Kershaw Alaskan Blade Traders, and living off the land, nibbling plump, juicy huckleberries. We did walk out of the woods long enough to listen to Oregon kick the living snot out of Michigan, which proved a welcome distraction from the deer-less drudgery. At the end of the weekend, we cased our guns and drove home in disgust, leaving our lonely tent trailer provisioned with all the clean clothes and hearty hunting food such as Pop Tarts and Teddy Grahams that we would need for the following weekend.

I figured to arrive in camp the following Friday to find the tent trailer already set up, and all the provisions ready to roll. My only worry was that wild hairy beasts would lay waste to the to trailer, motivated either by hunger or orneriness.

When we returned the following Friday in the dark, I held my breath as we pulled into camp and the headlights revealed the tent trailer none the worse for wear. I exhaled a sigh of relief, and we took our guns and backpacks inside.

The first order of business was to stir up some soup, so I opened the top drawer in search of a match. I stared blankly at the contents of the drawer, which was packed with pink feathers.

"Darwin, did you spill a package of Teddy Grahams in this drawer?" I wanted to ask him if he had also plucked a flamingo, but stopped myself at just one stupid question.

I picked up the bag, which was empty, and had a one-inch hole centered near the bottom. Mice had visited us.

Further investigation revealed that the rodents had enjoyed a weeklong party in our absence, dining on our junk food, and making confetti out of anything they could chew. Even the paper towel roll on a horizontal wall rack had been shredded.

A now-featherless dust mop turned out to be the source of the bed the mice had made for themselves in the drawer, which they had made a cozy bed & breakfast with a winter's supply of Teddy Grahams.

We confined our food consumption to what was in cans and didn't sleep very well, wondering if the raiders would return to do more damage. Eventually, the alarm clock ripped into my sleep, and we set out again into the wilderness for another hapless hunt.

When we returned, we found evidence that the mice had paid another visit, probably delighted to find that we had made the beds and brought fresh food to restock their new digs.

Exhausted and disgusted, we cleaned the camper as best we could, and hitched it up. As we did, I hoped that those mangy mice had bailed out before we took the trailer down and sealed them up in it. The alternative was unthinkable. Just to be on the safe side, I set up the trailer in the garage when I got home. I wasn't worried about the possibility of the mice getting loose in my garage, because that would amount to little more than a trap-and-transplant release to bolster the resident population already residing in my garage. Hopefully, none of the indigenous garage mice seized the opportunity to make the trailer their winter home before I folded it up again. If they did, I guess I'll find out when I get back to camp.

—*Contributed by Dewey Delaney*

DEER HUNTING 101

MULTIPLE CHOICE QUESTIONS
FROM THE NATIONAL HUNTER EDUCATION TEST

IF YOU PLAN TO HUNT PRIVATE PROPERTY, YOU SHOULD:

1. Tell the owner the date and time of your hunt.
2. For safety's sake, shoot at the barn from your stand to see if the bullet goes that far.
3. Leave the gate open so the cattle can free-range to bring higher market prices.
4. Offer to take the farmer's daughter to the Saturday dance down at the Grange.
5. Bring chocolate and nylons to the farmer's wife. If that fails, bring a new cotton dress.
6. Offer the landowner the heart, liver, brains, and bone marrow of your game.
7. All the above.
8. None of the above except 4.

WHEN YOU ARE ESTIMATING THE DISTANCE TO A TARGET, YOU SHOULD KEEP:

1. One eye open.
2. One eye shut.
3. Both eyes open.
4. One mind open.
5. Your pants up.
6. Her pants down.
7. All the above.
8. None of the above except 6.

WHICH OF THE FOLLOWING ITEMS SHOULD BE ON YOUR DEER HUNTING CHECKLIST, REGARDLESS OF THE KIND OF HUNTING PLANNED?

1. Toilet paper, a Costco 24-pack if you sit on a deer stand.
2. iPod loaded with Da Yoopers deer hunting music.
3. iPhone loaded with old girlfriend's numbers.
4. Small game license if you plan to take a small deer.
5. Knife or, where available, a chainsaw.
6. Moisture-wicking underwear.
7. Odor-eating underwear.
8. All the above especially 7.

IF YOU HAVE ONLY ONE SHOT, WHERE SHOULD YOU AIM ON A DEER?

1. Behind the right shoulder.
2. Behind the left shoulder
3. Not on the right rump roast.
4. Not on the left rump roast.
5. Up the "O" ring.
6. Between the eyes.
7. All the above near your brother-in-law's stand when he is sleeping or taking a dump.

DRIVING DEER IS AN EFFECTIVE TECHNIQUE TO COVER LARGE AREAS AND CONSISTS OF:

1. One hunter driving and second hunter shooting out the rear window.
2. One hunter driving/shooting and second shooting out the front windows.
3. One hunter and his family shooting out all windows.
4. One hunter driving, second hunter and both families shooting out all windows and moon roof.
5. One hunter driving (pushing) deer through cornfield and eating dirt sandwich within range of the blockers.

SCENT CONTROL IS CRITICAL ON A DEER STAND. WHEN ARE DEER MORE LIKELY TO SMELL YOU?

1. After a big breakfast of bacon, eggs, grits, French toast, and coffee.
2. After your big post-breakfast dump.
3. Before your big pre-lunch dump.
4. After your big post-lunch dump.
5. After your second big post-lunch dump
6. After your big pre-dinner dump.
7. When you stand next to your brother-in-law
8. All the above.

A HUNTER FROM BROWNSVILLE, TEXAS was on his first Alaska hunt. We were going around the hill one morning and he didn't want to be up there. Flatlanders rarely know what to do when confronted with Alaska's hills. We were going around a hill when his horse kicked a rock loose. It went down the mountain, gaining speed as it tumbled. I told him, "That's exactly what would happen if you fell off."

I shouldn't have said that. I left him there to hunt down to the meadow a half a mile away. While the horses fed, I sat in the meadow and waited. I took my field glasses and looked for him. He was on all fours, backing down the hill and looking over his shoulder for falling rocks.

—*Contributed by Rhett Bradford*

AT THE HOSPITAL, BUFORD TRIED to explain to the police sergeant why his cousin shot him.

"Yuh," he began. "We wuz having a good time drinking beer, when cousin Billy Joe picked up his shotgun and said, 'Hey, do youse fellows wanner go hunting?'"

"Then what happened?" the officer interrupted.

"From what I remember," Buford said, "I stood up and said, 'I'm game.'"

IF WE WEREN'T MEANT TO EAT DEER, why are deer made of meat?

PLAYFUL PRANKS HAVE BECOME an art form in hunting camps, and they provide endless entertainment when there are no game animals around to break the monotony. I can truthfully say that practical jokes are about the only game you'll ever find in my camp.

I'm not talking about really mean practical jokes, like letting the air out of your buddy's tires the night before opening morning, or swapping his regular coffee for decaf. I'm talking about harmless stuff, like putting a rubber snake in his backpack. Plastic bugs are great, too. I'll put them on a buddy's pillow, or better yet, inside the sleeping bag so he feels them first, then has to bail out of the sack in the dark and flail around, trying to figure out what's bugging him. The best part about artificial creepy crawlers is that in the low light conditions of camp, they look even more evil and lifelike.

The trouble with jokes that involve props is that they always come back to get you. Once after leaving a rubber snake wrapped around my buddy Frank Casebeer's boot one evening, I had forgotten about it when I woke up in the morning. I stumbled out to use my camp potty chair, only to find the snake coiled around one of the legs of the chair. Mind you, I didn't notice the rubber reptile until after I had sat down.

Of course, there's much worse than paybacks. I arrived at my hunting stand one morning to find a scorpion on the stump I always sit on. I was annoyed enough by the prank, but even more appalled that Frank knew where my hunting spot was. I reached down in disgust to put the dumb thing in my pocket, and almost did a back flip when it scurried off the stump. I never gave Frank the satisfaction of knowing he got me without trying.

The key to a good prank is imagination, and you can find inspiration anywhere. Once when my wife Dorey was dredging the chick flick section of the local video store, I talked the clerk out of a cardboard cutout of Bigfoot that was promoting the *Harry and the Hendersons* movie. When we were camped at the Elkhorn

Wildlife Area a couple seasons ago, Bigfoot was waiting for Frank in the outhouse.

You never want to be the first to fall asleep or the last to wake up in camp, and it's best to sleep with one eye open. A classic is to squirt shaving cream into each of a sleeping buddy's hands, and then tickle his face with a feather until he plasters himself.

One time Frank realized there were no mirrors in camp, and after an entire week, it seemed every hunter I encountered acted as though I were a crazed leper. I returned home to discover my face sported a handlebar mustache and Frankenstein stitches drawn with a permanent marker. I guess Frank thought that was a payback for when I had put shoe polish on the eyepieces of his binoculars so he had two black eyes the whole trip.

A good one he did was when he popped up one morning, turned off his alarm clock, set it two hours ahead, and put it in the bottom of my backpack. How he knew I'd be nodding off about 8 AM on my stand I'll never know.

Being from West London, Steve has a crude sense of humor, probably a product of the pubs. When I picked up my last set of hunting pictures, I got a really odd look from the clerk, who didn't want to touch the money I gave her. When I got to the car, I started thumbing through the photos only to discover a blurry picture of Steve's—let's just say it wasn't his best side.

But the classic from this past season had to be when Frank tied a rope from my potty chair to my back bumper on opening morning of deer season. I drove off into the darkness, and when I looked in my rearview mirror, I saw something chasing me in the red light of my taillights. Still groggy from sleep depravation and spooked by this odd object hot on my tail, I hit the gas, but the thing only accelerated to match my pace and leapt even more wildly. I began evasive maneuvers, trying to shake my pursuer, but the thing made every corner, every turn, and never lost a step.

Finally I hit a bar ditch, which just about dislodged the Rambler from its chassis and my head from my shoulders. When

I regained control, I saw the demon hit the bar ditch and spin out, flying over the edge of the road, crashing into a tall fir trunk and disappearing into the dark canyon below.

"Ha!" I yelled in triumph as I sped away into the darkness. "Don't mess with Dewey!"

—*Contributed by Dewey Delaney*

THE GUIDEBOOKS OF FAMOUS OUTFITTER, George Herter, contain some of the best pieces of outdoor humor ever. How can you argue with snippets like these, from his *Professional Guides Manual:*

•If the deer stand is one that deer will approach from more than one direction, two men are much better on a stand and permit no fires on deer stands.

•Do not take heavyset clients on horseback hunts as riding a horse tends to make your stomach move up and down. On a client that is real heavyweight, his whole belly will bob up and down, which will affect his heart.

•If a member of your party remains in camp while you and your clients are out hunting, have him blow a note or two on a bugle every half-hour, to keep them from becoming seriously lost.

Herter even has home advice for keeping deer out of your garden: "Write to the nearest zoo for a sack of lion manure, either African or North American. Scatter the lion manure around the edge of your garden and no deer will go near it."

Dear Reader: Please let me know how this tip works for you.

THREE BUCKS ARE IN A MOUNTAIN meadow complaining. A huge buck has entered their area and they aren't happy about sharing any of their does.

The Alpha buck says, "Since we've settled our differences and split up the does, I've been happy with my 30 does. I'm not about to share any with this new buck."

The second toughest buck says, "I only have 20 does, so I can't afford to share any of mine."

The youngest buck says, "I may be half as big as you guys, but I'm not going to give up any of my 10 does."

Suddenly the biggest, baddest buck appeared at the edge of the meadow. He weighed close to 375 pounds, and with huge sweeping antlers. As the huge buck trotted toward the three other bucks the ground seemed to shake.

Suddenly the former Alpha buck is a bit more flexible. "Maybe I could spare a few does."

The second toughest buck says, "Maybe if I hide in the bushes, he'll leave me alone."

But the small, young buck is snorting, raking the brush, and shaking his fledgling antlers in an extremely confrontational way. Worried about the reckless youngster, the two older bucks trot over to the young buck and say, "Listen, son. It's not worth dying for. Just give the new buck your does."

"He can have my does," replies the young buck, shaking his antlers again. "I'm just making sure he knows I'm a buck!"

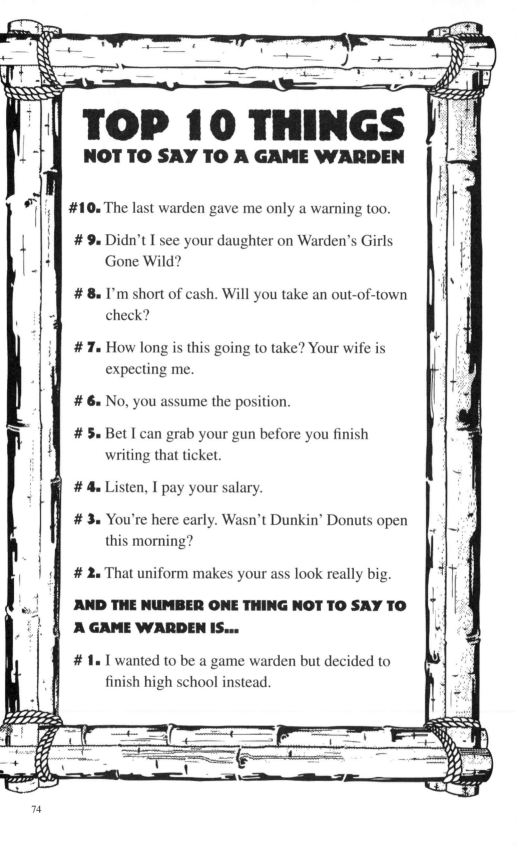

TOP 10 THINGS
NOT TO SAY TO A GAME WARDEN

#10. The last warden gave me only a warning too.

 # 9. Didn't I see your daughter on Warden's Girls Gone Wild?

 # 8. I'm short of cash. Will you take an out-of-town check?

 # 7. How long is this going to take? Your wife is expecting me.

 # 6. No, you assume the position.

 # 5. Bet I can grab your gun before you finish writing that ticket.

 # 4. Listen, I pay your salary.

 # 3. You're here early. Wasn't Dunkin' Donuts open this morning?

 # 2. That uniform makes your ass look really big.

AND THE NUMBER ONE THING NOT TO SAY TO A GAME WARDEN IS...

 # 1. I wanted to be a game warden but decided to finish high school instead.

A DEER HUNTER WAS SPENDING A WEEK

road hunting in Nevada. After seeing many billboards for houses of ill repute, he couldn't stand it anymore and pulled into the nearest cathouse. The madam at the door inquired, "Can I help you?" The deer hunter replied, "I need fulfillment of an urgent desire. Money is no object. $1000 or more is not a problem."

"How can we completely fulfill your urgent desire?" asked the madam.

"I want the biggest, fattest, ugliest, foul-mouthed woman you have and a baloney sandwich."

"For that money, I can set you up with a beautiful woman trained in all the ancient arts of pleasure and the largest steak in the country."

The deer hunter responded, "I didn't stop here because I'm horny. I pulled over because I'm homesick."

"Somehow they seem to know the season doesn't open til tomorrow."

A CHICAGO TENDERFOOT READS in *Field & Stream* about the challenges and excitement of hunting deer in the Wisconsin northwoods and decides to try it for himself. He rushes to the sporting goods store and buys himself a rifle, ammo, and all the clothing and gear necessary for his adventure. He drives north to the cabin he has booked over a November weekend and falls asleep that night with big antlered bucks prancing through his dreams. Next morning he's out early and stations himself behind a tree near a game trail. Before long, a large boar black bear comes walking down the path. The tenderfoot immediately reasoned that, while not a deer, this certainly was a northwoods trophy worth shooting. He quickly raised his rifle and fired.

The bullet sailed wildly over the startled bear who immediately charged. The tenderfoot ran terrified back to the cabin and slammed the door behind him. Seconds later the door opened and there stood the angry bear. The tenderfoot cowered in fear as the bear attacked, mauling the hunter and tearing off his pants. The tenderfoot screamed in pain as the bear violated him from behind.

Shortly thereafter the bear left the cabin leaving the tenderfoot an angry, ashamed, bloody mess. He vowed to get even with the bear and set out next morning with his rifle and stood behind the same tree along the same trail. Soon the bear appeared. The tenderfoot took careful aim, fired, and missed the bear once again. He raced in terror back to the cabin with the bear chasing and closing fast. Reaching the cabin he slammed the door behind him and watched in horror as the door flew open and the bear attacked, repeated the mauling and violation of the previous day, then left.

Despite his painful wounds, the tenderfoot was so angry that next morning he limped to the same tree along the same trail. When the bear showed up, he fired, missed, ran back to the cabin and slammed the door behind him. Momentarily the door opened and there stood the bear who gave the tenderfoot a wry look and said, "You're not really here for the hunting are you."

HUNTERS IN THE DEER CAMP AGREED that there would no whining about the quality of the camp cooking and, should there be any grumbling, the complainer would become the new cook. Nobody wanted to cook as the job took time away from the stand.

But Jake had been camp cook too long. One day while hunting in the woods, he picked up some deer scat for the evening meal.

That night after a hard day, the hunters returned to a big pot of Jake's big buck stew.

Digging in, Bob suddenly spit out the secret ingredient. "Deer shit!" he said and quickly added, "Good, though."

"SO YOU WANT A DAY OFF to go deer hunting? Let's look closely at your request. There are 365 days per year available for work. There are 52 weeks per year in which you already have two days off per week. That leaves 261 days available for work. Since you spend 16 hours each day away from work, you have used up 170 days, leaving only 91 days available for work. You spend 30 minutes each day on coffee breaks that account for 23 days each year, leaving only 68 days now available for work. With your one hour lunch breaks each day, you use up another 46 days, leaving only 22 days left for work. You normally spend 2 days a year on sick leave and this leaves you only 20 days to work. We close the plant for 5 holidays per year so your available working time is now down to 15 days. And once you use the 14 days vacation time each year, there is only 1 day available for you to work and I'll be dammed if you'll get that day off to go deer-hunting!"

STRANGE THINGS HAPPEN WHEN....
YOU SPEND NINE DAYS IN A TREE STAND

Add a month or more of bowhunting before and after gun season, not to mention ten days of muzzleloader season, and a guy is likely to go bonkers. On sunny days, shadows will play tricks with your eyes; on dreary, overcast days, time seems to stand still; and any day you might see more squirrels, turkeys and other hunters than deer.

After enough deer-less hours, every hunter's mind starts to wander. You might try to recall all the deer you have killed, or guess which direction the next one will come from. Some guys replay last week's football game, or imagine a wife or girlfriend in a seductive pose.

Me, I make up limericks. Don't ask me why. Maybe I'm nuts, but it passes the time and keeps me alert, as I watch for deer and search for new rhymes.

Here are a few from a recent deer season. Did I get a deer? Can't you tell?

WHEN YOU SIT WAY TOO LONG IN A TREE,
STRANGE THINGS YOU WILL HEAR AND YOU'LL SEE.
SIT THROUGH SNOW AND THROUGH RAIN,
IT'LL MESS WITH YOUR BRAIN,
AND YOU'LL START TO GO CRAZY – LIKE ME!

I'm amazed at how many different critters there are in the woods. When I hunted up north, I routinely saw ermine—weasels in their white winter coats—streaking through brown brush piles like fuzzy little snakes on steroids, and shrikes hovering low over meadows trying to catch voles. Once, a coyote trotted in and bedded down 50 yards from my tree. I figured he would spook any deer that came by, so I waved my hand and he took off. Another time, a goshawk landed in a nearby tree and stayed for an hour.

Elsewhere in Wisconsin, the critter parade is more mundane. And there's always a chance some foolhardy hiker will blunder past you, heedless of the season or its danger.

> **WHILE SITTING ALONE IN YOUR OAK,**
> **THE CRITTER PARADE IS A JOKE:**
> **FOUR RACCOONS AND A TURKEY,**
> **WHILE YOU CHAW ON BEEF JERKY,**
> **AND A HIKER WHO STOPS FOR A SMOKE.**

Try as you might to keep focused on the task at hand, distractions are everywhere. Pay too much attention to a non-target species, as intriguing as it may be, and you're likely to miss an opportunity at a deer. Who has not put his rifle down to pour a cup of coffee or take a bite of a sandwich, only to have a deer walk by at that instant?

> **ORANGE CAMOUFLAGE WORKS LIKE A CHARM**
> **'CAUSE A CHICKADEE LANDS ON YOUR ARM.**
> **THEN HE HOPS ON YOUR GUN,**
> **AND YOU THINK, 'THIS IS FUN,'**
> **WHILE A WHITETAIL SNEAKS PAST YOU UNHARMED.**

Some deer camps are notorious for partying all night, but who among us has not dozed off while hunting, even after a good night's sleep? I met a guy who fell from a tree stand and broke his neck because he couldn't stay awake after walking all day. When I saw him, he had one of those halo braces screwed into his skull to immobilize his neck. It's a good reason to wear a safety harness!

YOU CLIMB INTO YOUR TREE BEFORE DAWN,
AND YOU TRY ALL DAY LONG NOT TO YAWN.
IF PERCHANCE YOU SHOULD SNOOZE
FROM LAST NIGHT'S CARDS AND BOOZE,
WHEN YOU WAKE ALL THE DEER MAY BE GONE.

Limericks are all about meter and rhyme. They are usually nonsensical, often bawdy, and most end with a twist of logic or humorous punch line. They're pretty easy to write once you get the hang of it. The trick is to arrange your words in a "bada BOOM, bada BOOM, bada BOOM" beat. In poetic jargon, this is called "anapestic trimeter" (An anapest is a "foot" of poetry consisting of two unstressed syllables followed by one stressed syllable: bada BOOM; and "trimeter" is a line of verse consisting of three feet.), but that phrase didn't work here, so I used or abused poetic license.

One of the biggest challenges of limericks is keeping them G-rated. On a hunt up north a few years back, I had to make a pit stop, so I leaned my rifle against a nearby tree and did my business. I heard three shots, followed by hoof beats, and looked up to see a doe and a small buck running toward me. I had a doe tag and would have preferred to shoot her, but she got past me before I could grab my rifle, so I killed the buck in mid leap with a lung shot at 15 yards. I felt bad about it, but the season was ending and we had no venison yet.

I ONCE STOPPED ON A HUNT FOR MY EASE,
WHEN A BUCK TROTTED PAST THROUGH THE TREES.
I WAS DONE IN A TRIFLE,
SO I REACHED FOR MY RIFLE
AND SHOT HIM, MY PANTS 'ROUND MY KNEES.

My wife wonders when it will end, this limerick rut that I'm in. Guess I'll just have to quit before she has a fit. Oops, it's started all over again!

—*Contributed by Dan Small*

"Are you sure they didn't waste any?"

BEFORE HE WAS OLD ENOUGH TO HUNT,

my son Jon spent many hours in tree stands with me while I rattled, bleated, grunted, and waited, but neither luck nor skill ever brought a deer close enough for a shot while he was present. During one five-year period, I think I shot only one deer with a bow, and that was a doe. Jon was not impressed. Bowhunting bored him, but he liked the gadgets associated with the sport. When he finally came of age to hunt, he carried the rattling antlers and deer calls with him.

On the second day of the gun deer season, Jon and I were hunting a wooded hillside loaded with deer sign. Trails crisscrossed the area in several directions, and one spot near the top of the hill had so many scrapes and rubs it looked like a war zone. I sat at the edge of the woods along a power line right of way near a trail crossing while Jon picked a stand just off another trail near the biggest concentration of scrapes. He figured the closer to the action he could get, the better his chances.

The weather was calm and quite mild for November, and I dozed off a couple of times in the late afternoon sun. Around 4 PM I heard the sound of rattling antlers coming from Jon's direction.

Five minutes later he rattled again. There was something odd about the sound of his rattling, something vaguely familiar, yet not quite right. I couldn't pinpoint it. Then a single shot rang out and I jumped to my feet. Jon whistled loudly so I headed up the hill, hoping he had killed a buck. When I reached him, he was beaming over his first buck, a decent 8-pointer.

"Way to go, son," I said. "Now tell me how it happened."

"I sat there all afternoon without seeing anything. I knew it was getting late and I figured I had nothing to lose by rattling, so I tried a couple of times. Pretty soon I saw this deer coming down the trail. At first I thought it was a doe, but then I saw the rack."

"Did you have a clear shot?"

"Yeah, but he was coming right toward me so I thought I'd let him get closer to be sure I wouldn't miss. Then he stopped and made a scrape in the middle of the trail."

"Why didn't you shoot him then?"

"I'd never seen that before. He pawed at the ground with his front feet and peed down his hind legs over the scrape. Then he stretched his legs up and grabbed a branch in his mouth and broke it off. Boy, was that ever neat. Have you ever seen that, Dad?"

I told him that I hadn't and I grew envious as well as proud.

"I was afraid I'd spook him if I moved, so I sat still and figured I'd shoot him when he got past me."

The buck had other plans, though, and veered off the path before he reached Jon.

"When he swung around behind me, I thought he might get away. As I turned, he heard me move and froze, so I aimed at his chest and fired. He ran ten yards and piled up under a tree."

The buck lay where he had fallen, shot through the heart. As we field dressed him, I remembered the unusual rattling pattern and asked Jon what he had done to call in the buck. He shrugged and looked at me sheepishly.

"I had this song from one of my favorite Guns 'N Roses tapes in my head all afternoon, so I just banged the antlers together to the rhythm of that song."

"What was the song?" I asked.

" 'Rocket Queen' from *Appetite for Destruction*."

I'd always suspected that kind of music dangerous, but now here was irrefutable proof. It's a good thing its power was aimed in the right direction.

—*Contributed by Dan Small*

POLICE FILES

The Oregon State Police Fish & Wildlife Division waited for the deer season to open since this was also the opening of poaching season. Officers set up their decoy of an eight-point buck well before daylight and the start of legal shooting time, and waited in the comfort of their heated cars. They got quite a few people that morning, many claiming that the buck was too good to pass up. One poacher carried seven different guns in his rig, from a .22 to shotguns to pistols. He shot the decoy with three of the seven guns before the officers stopped him. Besides being early, he only had a doe tag. They confiscated his guns and gave him a ticket. The decoy was left standing after daylight for a couple of hours to catch any road hunters, and they went to pick it up after they wrote a bunch more tickets. Here came the same poacher. He pulled up to the officers and said, "I figured I better go home and get another gun and fill my doe tag on account of I won't be hunting for a while."

ON THE FIRST NIGHT AT THE large hunting lodge, two of the newest members were being introduced to other hunters. Knowing the newbies were anxious to be part of the group, the man handling the introductions said, "If you want to hear good deer hunting stories, ask that old gentleman asleep in the big chair by the fireplace. He's a senior member of the camp and knows stories you won't forget."

So they woke the old duffer and asked him for a hunting story.

"Well, boys, I'll tell you about a deer hunt back in the 40's up in northern Canada. My buddy and I had been hunting hard for four days, on foot, separately stalking and didn't see a darn thing. On the fifth day, I was so tired that mid-day; I just had to rest my legs. So I found a blown down tree, laid my gun down, propped myself in a comfortable position and quickly fell asleep. I don't know how long I was asleep "'but I do remember the big noise in the bushes that woke me up. I was grabbing my rifle when the biggest buck I ever saw jumped out of the brush like this:

WHHHHHHHHOOOOOOOOOOOOOAHHHHH!!!' I tell you, I just filled my pants."

The young men looked at each other and one said, "I don't blame you at all, I would have filled my pants if that had happened to me too."

The old duffer just shook his head and said, "No, not then, just now when I said 'WHHHHHHOOOOOOOOOOOOOAHHHHH!!!!'"

ONE SATURDAY MORNING, a deer hunter gets up early, puts on his long johns and camouflage clothing, makes his lunch, grabs his rifle, and goes out to the garage to warm up his rig and head to his favorite deer woods.

As the deer hunter heads out of his garage, rain pounds on his truck. Snow and sleet is mixed with the rain and the wind is howling. He decides to go back in the house to check the weather channel: it's going to be like this all day. He puts his truck back in the garage, stashes his rifle, and quietly undresses and slips back into bed.

Under the covers, he cuddles up to his wife's back in a comfortable spoon and whispers, "The weather out there is really crummy." To which she sleepily replies, "Can you believe my dumb ass husband is out hunting in that shit?"

"Hope Mom doesn't get too lonesome while we're gone."

LARS AND OLE GO DEER HUNTING and Lars accidentally shoots Ole. He rushes Ole to the hospital and after a long surgery, the doctor comes out and says, "Lars, we could have saved Ole if you wouldn't have field dressed him first."

A LOT OF HUNTERS CARRY A BOTTLE into the stand for use as a urinal. My favorite is an old hot water bottle; I need the wide mouth variety that is hard to find these days. Here's a great idea to pull on an unsuspecting hunting partner. When no one is looking, crush up four or five Alka-Seltzer tablets and slip the resulting powder into his bottle. Just stand back and deny your guilt.

—Contributed by Barry Wensel

MY COLLEGE ROOMMATE, BOB, told me about a bowhunter who made a lucky "Texas heart shot." This fellow drew on a buck that turned and ran just as he let the arrow fly. The hunter watched as the deer raced off through the woods and then fell dead. When he went to field dress the deer, there wasn't a mark on it. It was as though the buck had died of fright or something. When he opened up the buck, though, it looked like a grenade had gone off in its guts. His arrow had scored a bull's eye on the buck's behind, entering its rectum, and plowing through its innards to lodge in its heart.

—Contributed by Dan Small

WHEN IT COMES TO HUNTING LUCK, Jon just lives right. On his first Western hunt he had downed a near-record-book antelope with one shot and doubled on drake mallards. The next deer season, though, Jon got a rude taste of reality. On opening morning, a small forkhorn crossed the gas pipeline cut he was watching. He had it in his sights but let it walk, since the season was young and he was in the big buck pool at the local sporting goods store. Later that morning I made a drive toward him through a small wood lot and heard deer running and snorting as I approached his stand, so I stopped and waited. Several minutes I heard a shot, then another, then a third. A large-bodied deer ran past me but snow-covered brush obscured its head and I didn't shoot.

"I got him, Dad, a big one!" Jon yelled. "Did you see him?"

I hurried out to the clearing and found Jon bug-eyed with excitement.

"What happened?"

"You pushed three deer across the pipeline behind me: a doe, a spike buck and a monster buck—a ten-pointer at least," he said. "They crossed too quickly for me to shoot but I heard them stop just inside the woods so I grunted a couple of times on my deer call. The little spike crossed back over but I let him go. I grunted again and the does crossed. All this time I could hear the big buck stomping and snorting in the woods so I grunted once more. Then he walked out and stood broadside right down there."

He gestured toward the buck's tracks, not 40 yards from his stand.

"I shot him but he just stood there so I shot him again but he still didn't move. When I shot him a third time he ran back toward you. You didn't find him in there?"

"No, but let's check his trail."

We easily found where the buck had been standing and where Jon's three shots had hit the snow under the buck's belly, but there was not a trace of hair or blood. Just to be sure we followed his track a quarter-mile through the woods, but he never slowed and there was no sign that he had been hit.

"I'm afraid you missed him clean," I said. "I guess you were already spending the buck pool money instead of concentrating on your aim."

"Man, he was big," Jon said. "And he was so close I even heard him fart."

—Contributed by Dan Small

LARS AND OLE GO DEER HUNTING and Lars accidentally shoots Ole. He rushes Ole to the hospital and after a long surgery, the doctor comes out and says, "Lars, we could have saved Ole if you hadn't taken so much time tying him to the hood of your car."

WHAT'S THE DIFFERENCE BETWEEN Beer Nuts and deer nuts? Beer Nuts are around a dollar seventy-nine, and deer nuts are just under a buck.

A FELLOW TAKES OFF FOR HIS annual deer hunting trip up north. When he returns home, he's upset with his wife, saying "you forgot to pack my underwear!" Her reply; "I put your underwear in your gun case."

A 110-YEAR-OLD MAN is having his annual checkup. The doctor asks him how he's feeling.

"I've never felt better," he replies. "I've got an eighteen-year-old bride who's pregnant with my child. What do you say to that?"

The doctor thinks for a moment and says, "Let me tell you a story. I know a man who's an avid hunter. He never misses a season but one day he's in a bit of a hurry and accidentally grabs his umbrella instead of his gun. He's walking in the woods near a creek and suddenly spots a deer in the brush in front of him. He raises the umbrella, points it at the deer, squeezes the handle, and BAM! The deer drops dead in front of him."

That's impossible," said the old man in disbelief. "Someone else must have shot that deer!"

"Exactly," said the doctor.

AN EXHAUSTED DEER HUNTER in the Northern Michigan wilderness stumbles upon another hunter and his small camp. "Boy, am I glad to see you!" said the hunter. "I've been lost for three days."

"Don't get too excited," the other hunter replied. "I've been lost for three weeks."

DEFINITION OF A NON-TYPICAL WHITETAIL:
One that doesn't cross the road.

THE WEDNESDAY-NIGHT CHURCH SERVICE
coincided with the last day of hunting season. The pastor asked
who had bagged a deer and no one raised a hand. Puzzled, the
pastor said, "I don't get it. Last Sunday many of you said you were
missing because of hunting season. I had the whole congregation
pray for your deer."

One hunter groaned, "Well, it worked. They're all safe."

TWO LAWYERS WERE OUT HUNTING when they
came upon a couple of tracks. After close examination, the first
lawyer declared them to be deer tracks. The second lawyer dis-
agreed, insisting they must be elk tracks. They were still arguing
when the train hit them.

WE WERE HUNTING ON A RIDGE in Swan Valley,
Idaho, and the snow was about crotch deep. A buck stood about
four hundred yards away, and my partner shot him. It fell over and
we had to pick our way through ledges and rocks to get to him. My
partner said, "Let me clean it."

The buck was puffed up pretty good and I decided to let him.
He had gut-shot it. He stood between the hind legs and stuck his
knife into the paunch. Green stuff and gas hit him in the face. He
fell over in the snow and heaved, and heaved, and heaved. I was
laughing pretty hard. He turned around with tears streaming down
his face and said, "That almost made me sick."

—*Contributed by Rhett Bradford*

A TYPICAL DAY
IN THE DEER STAND IN NORTHERN MINNESOTA

HALF HOUR BEFORE SUNRISE: Walk blindly into woods, climb into stand.

NEXT HOUR: Wait for your overheated sweat machine to soak your clothes.

NEXT HOUR: Go big job.

NEXT HOUR: Fantasize about your secretary.

NEXT HOUR: Check safety. Watch squirrels play with their nuts.

NEXT HOUR: Fantasize about high school sweetheart.

NEXT HOUR: Check safety again. Watch blue jays play.

NEXT HOUR: Pre-lunch preparations. Lunch. Post-lunch clean up.

NEXT HOUR: Check safety. Watch geese fly over.

NEXT HOUR: Fantasize about boss being caught in bathroom scandal.

NEXT HOUR: Go big job.

NEXT HOUR: Check safety. Watch porcupine lumber across landscape.

NEXT HOUR: Fantasize about last night's barmaid.

HALF HOUR BEFORE SUNSET: Climb out of stand, walk out of woods, hoping to get out before night falls and dying lost in woods.

PS: If you start fantasizing about your ex-wife, you are allowed to leave the stand early or take a bonus big job.

EMERY HAD JUST FINISHED TELLING HOW

he acquired the bear skin that had hung on the cabin wall since 1964. He told the story once during every one of the subsequent deer seasons. It was an old story, but Emery enjoyed telling it, and we all enjoyed listening to it. The old ones are the best ones.

There was a pause in the conversation.

"Too bad about that hunter down at Gresham last year."

"Was there some trouble?"

"I don't believe I heard about it."

"What happened?"

"You must have seen it. It was in all of the papers."

"Not all of us get the *Shawano Evening Leader,* Floyd. What happened?"

Well, this diplomat—I believe he was a member of the Czecho-slovakian Consulate in Chicago—was a consummate deer hunter. According to the story; he had hunted with a group out of Gresham for five or six years and knew his way around the woods.

"Apparently he and his campmates formed a very close-knit group. It was like this camp. Everyone looked out for everyone else.

"Remember the cold snap at the end of last year's season? It must have gotten down to ten below. No civilized person would hunt in such teeth-shattering conditions. The diplomat suited up and walked out towards his stand. Like I say, he was a consummate deer hunter.

"During the evening meal, at about seven o'clock when the meat was all gone, someone noticed an empty chair at the table. After discussion, it was decided the consular official was the one who was missing. By ten o'clock, some of his campmates thought he may have been lost.

"They drove a few of the roads around their hunting territory and blew the horn, but heard no response—possibly because the windows in the car were rolled up in order to keep the occupants toasty warm. (It was still a bit below zero outside—a temperature they considered to be far too cold for a foot-search of the area.)

"The following morning the thermometer had climbed to a more pleasant 35 degrees, and after a leisurely noon luncheon (and a vote of five in favor and four against) a search team was organized. When the hunters arrived at the diplomats usual stand, a scene of bloody gore assaulted their eyes.

"They found a rifle with a broken stock, bits of flesh and blood-soaked clothing, one tooth-marked and lacerated boot, and the foot prints of two bear. The disturbed red snow gave evidence of the terrible fight that must have occurred. Of course, the hunters tracked down the two animals and dispatched them.

"Feeling they should give the Czech's remains a decent burial, his campmates opend the sow and searched her stomach contents. No trace of the diplomat was found. Then they turned their attention to the other beast and, sure enough, the Czech was in the male."

Reprinted from the book, That Reminds Me of the One…,
© 1995 Willow Creek Press by Galen Winter.

A PROFESSOR AT THE UNIVERSITY of Wisconsin was giving a lecture on "Involuntary Muscular Contractions" to his first year medical students. Realizing this was not the most riveting subject, the professor decided to lighten the mood slightly. He pointed to a young woman in the front row and asked, "Do you know what your asshole is doing while you're having an orgasm?"

"Probably deer hunting with his buddies," she replied.

It took 45 minutes to restore order in the classroom.

—Contributed by Very Anonymous with mea culpa to the more polite members in the deer camp.